Ignatius of Loyola Speaks

Other titles of interest from St. Augustine's Press

Ignatius of Loyola Speaks

KARL RAHNER, S.J.

Translated by Annemarie S. Kidder

ST. AUGUSTINE'S PRESS
South Bend, Indiana

Original publication of Karl Rahner's "Rede des Ignatious von Loyola an einen Jesuiten von heute" was taken from Rahner's *Ignatious von Loyola*, published by by Verlag Herder GmbH Translation copyright © 2013 by Annemarie S. Kidder

Manufactured in the United States of America

1 2 3 4 5 6   18 17 16 15 14 13

Library of Congress Cataloging in Publication Data
Rahner, Karl, 1904–1984.
[Rede des Ignatious von Loyola an einen Jesuiten von heute.
English]
Ignatius of Loyola speaks / Karl Rahner, S.J.;
translated by Annemarie S. Kidder.
pages cm
Includes index.
ISBN 978-1-58731-386-8 (paperbound : alk. paper) –
ISBN 978-1-58731-387-5 (e-book)
1. Ignatius, of Loyola, Saint, 1491–1556.
I. Kidder, Annemarie S. II. Title.
BX4700.L7R3213 2013
255'.53 – dc23   2012040208

∞ The paper used in this publication meets the minimum requirements of the American National Standard for Information Sciences Permanence of Paper for Printed Materials, ANSI Z39.481984.

ST. AUGUSTINE'S PRESS
www.staugustine.net

Introduction

It is well known that Karl Rahner, S.J. (1904–1984) ranks among the most influential theologians of our time. His bibliography includes more than sixteen hundred entries in German alone, spanning editorials, essays, lectures, sermons, prayers, book reviews, dictionary entries, and books on prayer, penance, the spiritual life, Ignatius of Loyola's *Exercises* and spirituality, and systematic theology. His contributions to the Second Vatican Council (1963–1965) shaped the doctrinal formulations on the church, the sacraments, and the role of the laity in the Roman Catholic Church. And his efforts at reconciling the scholastic approach to church doctrine with an existential, transcendental, and anthropological understanding of humanity's relationship with God earned him the reputation of having opened doors for ecumenical dialogue and intentionally engaging a scientific worldview and those outside the church.

Less well known is that toward the end of his life,

Rahner had slipped into the role of Ignatius of Loyola in an essay, titled "Speech of Ignatius of Loyola to a Modern-Day Jesuit." In doing so, Rahner not only proved that he could readily identify with the spirit of the sixteenth-century reformer and founder of the Society of Jesus, Rahner's order for more than sixty years; he also had summarized and clarified his own theological position and its mooring in the theological, mystical, and missionary heritage of the Jesuits, later calling the speech his "last will" or "testament."

Rahner had joined the Jesuits in 1922, professed final vows in 1939, and remained a Jesuit until his death in 1984. Only three weeks after his final examination in high school, he had entered the novitiate of the Upper German Province of the Society of Jesus. At the Jesuit house in Vorarlberg, Austria, he devoted himself to questions of the spiritual life, the life and history of the order, and the study of spiritual classics. At the time, Rahner was not clear why he had wanted to become a Jesuit, though the example of his brother Hugo, who had joined the order three years earlier, had undoubtedly made an impression on him. Two years later, his first article appeared, titled "Why We Need to Pray" (1924), possibly a result of the order's focus on prayer and a personal relationship with God in Christ.

After his philosophical studies, Rahner went on to study theology at the Jesuit order's school in Valkenburg, the Netherlands. The renewal movement among the Jesuits of the first half of the century showed a burgeoning interest in Ignatius and the *Exercises*. To that end, both Karl and Hugo Rahner collaborated, seeking to reaffirm the spiritual foundation of the Jesuits by a theology of prayer in the *Exercises*. According to Herbert Vorgrimler, one of Rahner's first doctoral students and a keen interpreter of Rahner's theology, "It was out of this concern that Karl Rahner's first major publications emerged in 1932 and 1933: about the doctrine of the spiritual senses in Origen and Bonaventure and the spiritual teaching of Evagrius Ponticus."[1] The same can be said about Rahner's dissertation, which though rejected by the doctoral supervisor, Martin Honecker, was published in 1939 as *Geist in Welt: Zur Metaphysik der endlichen Erkenntnis bei Thomas von Aquin* and translated into many languages, including into English as *Spirit in the World*. As Karl Heinz Neufeld, s.j. has said, Rahner's thoughts in *Spirit in the World* are mostly grounded "in concern with the practice of prayer among the Jesuits, just as conversely the significance of the senses for knowledge in Thomas Aquinas is part of the idea that the human senses have their irreplaceable value in [one's conversation] with God."[2] This Ignatian orientation and concern with prayer in Rahner appears in a 1937 lecture on Ignatius given in Vienna, where he explores Ignatius's mysticism,

1 Herbert Vorgrimler, *Understanding Karl Rahner: An Introduction to His Life and Thought* (New York: Crossroad, 1986), p. 57.
2 See Ibid.

monastic piety, and theology of the cross. It is also apparent in the 1938 collection of prayers, *Worte ins Schweigen* ("Words Spoken unto Silence") and published in English as *Encounters With Silence*. The silence is, of course, the Silent One, God. Later, Rahner would affirm the key role of Ignatian spirituality to him when experiencing it in the order: "The spirituality of Ignatius himself which we shared in through the practice of prayer and a religious formation has become more significant for me than all learned philosophy and theology inside and outside the Order."[3]

Early on and for more than twenty years, Rahner immersed himself in the great spiritual masters and mystics of the church's tradition. His intense studies are well documented by several hundred book reviews, essays, and lectures produced during that time frame, beginning with his first publications in the early 1930s. Much of this foundational work remained invisible to the larger public. Accumulated diligently into the sum total of a vast reservoir, his knowledge was never displayed for show or bedazzlement. However, it remained accessible and could be quickly recalled. In the words of Karl Cardinal Lehmann, Rahner's knowledge was "deposited as if on the quieter bottom of the sea and is waiting there, but immediately is ready when awakened by certain questions, when called upon and called on to proof

3   *Karl Rahner im Gespräch*, eds. Paul Imhof, S.J. and Hubert Biallowons, vol. II (Munich: Kösel Verlag, 1983), p. 51; in Vorgrimler, p. 57.

itself. Then they all appear: Irenaeus, Origen, the Cappadocians, Augustine, Thomas Aquinas, Bonaventure, Suárez, and last but not least the great mystics,"[4] including Ignatius of Loyola.

For much of Rahner's career, the general public regarded the "s.j." after his name as a private, hence relatively insignificant affair. This oversight was corrected when on the occasion of his eightieth birthday in 1984, a few weeks before his death, Rahner gave a speech at the University of Freiburg. Titled "Experiences of a Catholic Theologian," the speech identifies as the third of four points critical to his theological enterprise his life in the Jesuit order. "I, for one, hope that my great father of the order, Ignatius of Loyola, would agree that in my theology there is visible a little of his spirit and his unique spirituality." In fact, Rahner expressed "the rather immodest opinion" in the speech "that on this or that point I am nearer to Ignatius than the great Jesuit theology of the Baroque era, which did not always and certainly not in the significant points do sufficient justice to a legitimate existentialism in Ignatius (if one may be permitted to call it that)."[5]

4 Karl Cardinal Lehmann, "Karl Rahners Bedeutung für die Kirche" in *Stimmen der Zeit*, "Karl Rahner—100 Jahre," Spezial 1—2004, p. 11.

5 Karl Rahner, *Von der Unbegreiflichkeit Gottes: Erfahrungen eines katholischen Theologen*, ed. Albert Raffelt (Freiburg: Herder, 2004), p. 46; cf. *Sämtliche Werke*, vol. 25, *Erneuerung des Ordenslebens; Zeugnis für Kirche und Welt*, ed. Andreas R. Batlogg (Freiburg: Herder, 2008), p. 53.

Since then, a handful of academic studies have been published, all formerly dissertations, demonstrating that Rahner's theology cannot be properly understood or interpreted without taking into account his background as a Jesuit and his Ignatian spirituality. Among them might be mentioned the study on Rahner's "productive role model" Ignatius of Loyola by Arno Zalauer,[6] the significance of Ignatian spirituality to Rahner's thought by Philip Endean, S.J.,[7] and Rahner's interpretation and use of "The Mysteries of the Life of Jesus" (which are part of Ignatius's *Exercises*) in an attempt to make accessible the Christian faith by Andreas R. Batlogg, S.J.[8] As part of the 27-volume edition of the collected works of Karl Rahner, *Sämtliche Schriften*, an entire 700-page volume is dedicated solely to Ignatian themes.[9]

6   Arno Zalauer, *Karl Rahner und sein "produktives Vorbild" Ignatius of Loyola* (Innsbruck: Tyrolia, 1996).

7   Philip Endean, S.J., *Karl Rahner and Ignatian Spirituality.* New York, 2001; see also Philip Endean, S.J. "Introduction" in *Karl Rahner: Spiritual Writings*, edited with an introduction by Philip Endean, S.J. (New York: Maryknoll, 2004), pp. 9–30.

8   Andreas Batlogg, S.J., *Die Mysterien des Leben Jesu bei Karl Rahner. Zugang zum Christusglauben* (Innsbruck: Tyrolia, 2001).

9   See Karl Rahner, *Sämtliche Schriften*, vol. 13, *Ignatianischer Geist: Schriften zu den Exerzitien und zur Spiritualität des Ordensgründers* ("Ignatian Spirit: Writings on the Exercises and the Spirituality of the Order's Founder"), eds. Andreas

During his lifetime, Rahner made the Ignatian exercises regularly, twice the entire 30-day retreat. And he himself gave them. Between 1934 and 1984, Rahner offered the exercises more than fifty times to retreatants, Jesuits as well as seminarians. It is likely that Rahner would have offered them to a wider audience, as well, given different circumstances and times. After all, Ignatius had written the *Exercises* as a retreat manual for the retreat leader, so the exercises could be given to anyone wishing to draw closer to God. He himself had given them to virtually anyone who would ask. And when members of the Society of Jesus, founded in 1540, began serving as confessors and tutors to the nobility and had founded missions and schools, their charges were invited to make the exercises, either individually or in a group.

For Rahner as well as for Ignatius, the purpose of making the exercises was to discern the will of God for one's life, of making an "election," of being able to say "yes" to God in one's particular place and time in complete human freedom before God. Divided into four "weeks," or stages, the retreat based on the *Exercises* allows participants to see themselves in the light of God, to take account of their sins and the barriers that prevented them from experiencing God's presence with an opportunity for making confession after the first "week," thus, finding themselves before

R. Batlogg, Johannes Herzgsell, Stefan Kiechle (Freiburg: Herder, 2006).

the triune God in surrender and readiness to discern, hear, and perceive the divine self-communication meant for them. A fair share of the retreat time is spent in active imagination, prayer, and "colloquies," and in an immersion into the divine mysteries of Jesus' life, passion, death, and resurrection. From Rahner's perspective, Ignatius's *Exercises* are a preparation for and an invitation to a concrete encounter with Jesus Christ and the Trinitarian God. They make Ignatius somewhat of a Christian existentialist, someone who not only had received the graces of the mystic, replete with visions and ecstatic encounters (of which one finds frequent mentioning in Ignatius's diaries), but who also taught others how to enter into this mystical experience, how to come before the silent God in personal freedom and to be allowing for an authentic, "existential" meeting with God in the person of the loving, suffering Christ.

In 1978, Rahner was asked by the publisher Herder to write a piece for a pictorial monograph on Ignatius of Loyola. He agreed only because both leading experts on Ignatius, one of them his brother Hugo, had died years earlier. Instead of producing a descriptive synopsis of a historical figure, Rahner chose to slip into the role of Ignatius, assuming his persona and translating Ignatian terminology and ideals into modern speech and context. In essence, Rahner identified key elements and teachings of a great mystic, so they could assist modern-day seekers. Titled "Speech of Ignatius of Loyola to a Modern-

Day Jesuit,"[10] the speech is a spiritual tribute to the founder of the order and a reminder to modern-day Jesuits of their spiritual heritage, bringing into focus the Jesuit calling and responsibility in regard to the task of guiding souls. In addition, it is a contemporary theological testimony to the classic principles of Ignatian mysticism, a distillation of what mysticism aims for and where it invariably begins, namely in the personal, unmediated encounter with the mysterious, silent God, who chooses to reveal himself to the person. The speech is divided into fifteen sections, of which the first half addresses the origins and the nature of Ignatian mysticism, while the second offers encouragement and fresh perspectives to the order's members in their mission. To the general reader, the first four sections are of particular interest: they deal with Ignatius's "immediate experience of God," his desire to give "instruction" to others for gaining such an experience, a summary of his "spirituality," and the ways in which the personal God experience relates to the church as an institution.

In Rahner's view, Ignatius's personal experience with God is central to Ignatius's mission and mysticism: "You

10 Karl Rahner, "Rede des Ignatius von Loyola an einen Jesuiten heute" in *Ignatius von Loyola* (Freiburg: Herder, 1978), pp. 9–38; translated as "Ignatius of Loyola Speaks to a Modern Jesuit" in Karl Rahner, *Ignatius of Loyola*, with an historical introduction by Paul Imhof, S.J., color photographs by Helmut Nils Loose, and trans. by Rosaleen Ockenden (Cleveland: Collins, 1979), pp. 11–38.

know that I wanted to 'help souls,' as I called it then, telling people something about God and his grace and also about Jesus Christ, the crucified and risen one, so that their freedom would be freed unto the freedom of God. I wanted to say it in the same way as it has always been said in the church, and yet I felt that I could say the old in a new way, and that was true" (6). Repeatedly Rahner refers to Ignatius's God experience: "I have experienced God, the nameless and unfathomable one, the silent and yet near one, in the trinity of his love for me. I have experienced God also and most especially beyond all concrete imagery: the one who when drawing near of his own accord and out of sheer grace cannot be confused with anything else" (6). For "I have truly encountered God, the true and living one, the one who merits the name that extinguishes all others. Whether one wants to call this experience mysticism or something else is irrelevant here: how something like that can be made even remotely clear and put into human words is for your theologians to figure out" (7–8).

For Rahner, the Jesuits' primary responsibility in ministry is to help people come to a God experience. Ignatius offered the exercises "to whoever was open to such an offer of spiritual help" in the conviction that "God and the person can truly encounter each other in an immediate way" (10). This is "the essence of what you commonly call my spirituality" and may be "more closely related to the original experiences of Luther and Descartes than you Jesuits have been willing to admit over the centuries." Since people are able to truly experience God in their hearts, "your pastoral care should always and at every stage" be aware of this goal (11–12).

A look at the institutional church would suggest, according to Rahner, that "the church has constructed immense and complicated irrigation systems in order to water the soul of this heart and make it fertile by her word, her sacraments, her institutions, and guidelines for living." But in addition to these, "there [also] exists a deep well on this land itself, so that from this source, once drilled, bubble up on the land itself the waters of the living spirit unto eternal life." In fact, these "pipelines of grace from outside are of use only if they meet with the ultimate grace from within" (15–16).

Rahner's speech in the role of Ignatius received little attention during his lifetime. Published as part of a pictorial on Ignatius's life along with a historical sketch of the saint, the speech becomes buried amidst color plates and historical narrative. When asked to recount some light-hearted anecdotes at the celebration of his sixtieth jubilee year in the Jesuit order in 1982, Rahner told the following: "I had St. Ignatius give a speech to a modern-day Jesuit in a pictorial book on Ignatius. While I and a Protestant pastor[11] were having coffee in Rome with

11 At the time, the Protestant pastor and journalist Meinold Krauss was conducting an extensive television interview with Rahner on the upcoming occasion of the theologian's eightieth birthday; the interview also appeared in book format.

Superior General Arrupe [of the order], the latter asked me about the book. It's doing well, I said, and it has been translated into many languages. Yes, said Arrupe, the book has nice pictures."[12]

In 1983, a year before his death, Rahner called the essay on Ignatius "a sort of last will and testament." He had come to this conclusion some years after writing the speech and upon re-reading it. To Rahner, it contains the key themes of his theological enterprise and is "a résumé of my theology, in general, and of how I tried to live."[13]

This newly translated and annotated speech of Rahner's in the role of Ignatius seeks to offer readers two things, in particular: a fresh lens through which to reappraise the writings of one of the greatest theologians of our time, and a contemporary interpretation and application of the teachings and mysticism of Ignatius of Loyola for the present.

Annemarie S. Kidder

12 "Rahner-Worte und Geschichten" in Karl Rahner, *Sämtliche Werke*, vol. 25, *Erneuerung des Ordenslebens; Zeugnis für Kirche und Welt*, ed. Andreas R. Batlogg (Freiburg: Herder, 2008), p. 44.

13 Karl Rahner, *Faith in a Wintry Season: Interviews and Conversations with Karl Rahner in the Last Years of His Life, 1982–84*, eds. Hubert Biallowons, Harvey D. Egan, S.J., and Paul Imhof, S.J. (New York: Crossroad, 1990), p. 104.

Ignatius of Loyola Speaks

I, Ignatius of Loyola, want to try and say something about myself and the task of Jesuits today, provided they still feel obliged to my spirit and to that of my companions as it once defined this order. I don't intend to recount my life as in a historical biography. I have already given a brief account of my life[1] near its end in

1   At the urgings of his collaborators in the Society of Jesus, Ignatius of Loyola (1491–1556) gave a verbal account of his life in 1553 and 1555. The account spans eighteen of his sixty-five years, from Pamplona in 1521 through his first year in Rome in 1538. The recipient of Ignatius's story was Luis Gonçalves da Câmara, head of the Jesuit house in Rome. The purpose of the account was to show God's activity in developing Ignatius's spiritual and mystical life and how external events related to interior experiences. Unfortunately, the dictations were interrupted by Câmara's departure for Portugal in 1555, and the account was not completed at the time of Ignatius's death a year later. Câmara did not give a title to the manuscript, so that it ended up being called by various names: The Pilgrim's Story (because Ignatius had told his life's story by referring to himself in the third person and calling himself "the pilgrim"), Testament, or Autobiography.

the way I could see it then (in precisely that way) which
you still have; and beyond that, there have been plenty
of good and bad books written about me since then in
every century up to now. Instead, it is from the depths
of God's holy silence that I should like to speak and say
something about myself, though that is nearly impossible since what is spoken thus will transform from eternity into time again, even if time, too, is yet again
enveloped by the eternal mystery of God. And don't say
too quickly and easily that what I say can transform
from what is mine into yours; because for something to
be truly heard it has to reach your head and perhaps
your heart, too, thus carrying with it all the dubitable
traits of the listeners and the impermanence of their historical situation. As theologians you ought to know that
hearing is not everything and can even kill what is said.
Still, it is possible that as you are recording what you
hear from your end, something of what I wanted to say
is being preserved. And besides: If what I am going to
say now were to sound just like my words in the
Autobiography, in the *Exercises*,[2] in the

2   The *Spiritual Exercises*, commonly referred to as *Exercises*,
    is a small instruction manual on how to give spiritual exer-
    cises and practices to someone wishing to know how to
    please and serve God well. Ignatius began the composition
    of the book at Manresa in 1522 and at Barcelona, largely as
    notes to himself for carrying on spiritual conversations with
    others and enticing them to perform exercises of prayer, con-
    fession, and other activities to allow for a deepening of their

Constitutions[3]of my order and in the thousands of letters[4] I and my secretary Polanco[5] wrote together, if one could calmly take note of all of that as the mild wisdom of a saint, then I would be speaking only to my own time and not to yours.

spiritual life. Between 1522 and 1541, Ignatius continued to make additions and revisions to the manual, which was published in 1548.

3   The Constitutions of the Society of Jesus is the framework in which the order operates, and they show Ignatius's worldview regarding its organization, spirit, and governance. The Constitutions developed in stages: the first was the draft of 1539 aimed at obtaining papal approval of the order, which occurred in 1540, followed by some revisions; the second stage involved several expanded drafts and additions through the years, completed by 1552; the third and final stage was the draft made by Ignatius's secretary, Juan de Polanco, which was ratified in 1558 by the Society's First General Congregation.

4   Almost seven thousand of Ignatius's letters are extant and are published in twelve volumes. Fewer than two hundred of them predate March 1547, when Polanco became Ignatius's secretary.

5   In 1547, Ignatius had appointed Juan de Polanco as his secretary. Polanco (1517–1576) was born in Burgos, Spain, and went to study in Paris. After graduation, he went to Rome to work in the prestigious and lucrative position of scriptor apostolicus, an amanuensis with the papal curia. He joined the Jesuits in 1541 and in 1547 became the life-long secretary to Ignatius.

The Immediate God Experience

You know that I wanted to "help souls," as I called it then, telling people something about God and his grace and also about Jesus Christ, the crucified and risen one, so that their freedom would be freed unto the freedom of God. I wanted to say it in the same way as it has always been said in the church, and yet I felt that I could say the old in a new way, and that was true. Why? I was convinced that I had encountered God, at first in amateur-like fashion during my illness at Loyola and then decisively during my solitary time at Manresa, so that, as a result, I felt called to share this experience with others as much as possible.

When I insist on saying that I have experienced God, I have no need to tie this statement to a theological theorem on the nature of such an unmediated God experience, and it is not my intention either to talk about all the accompanying phenomena of such an experience, along with their inherent historical and individual intricacies. I am not talking about concrete visions, symbols, voices, the gift of tears, and similar things. All I am saying is this: I have experienced God, the nameless and unfathomable one, the silent and yet near one, in the trinity of his love for me. I have experienced God also and most especially beyond all concrete imagery: the one who when drawing near of his own accord and out of sheer grace cannot be confused with anything else.

Such a statement may sound rather harmless in this organization of yours that is run so piously and with as many high-sounding words as possible, but it is actually enormous: both from my perspective as I experienced the incomprehensibility of God so strangely and from the perspective of the godlessness of your own time where such godlessness merely eliminates the idols of a previous era that equated them in both harmless and terrible ways with the unfathomable God. Why should I not be allowed to say it: This godlessness also reaches into the church since throughout its history the church has meant to be the event where idols are being toppled in unity with the crucified one.

Were you never shocked to hear me say in my autobiography that my mysticism had given me such certainty of faith that it would have remained unshaken even in the absence of Holy Scripture? Would it not be easy to accuse me of subjective mysticism and heresy? Actually, I was not surprised at all that at Alcalá, Salamanca, and elsewhere I was suspected to be an Alumbrado.[6] I have truly encountered God, the true and

6   The name Alumbrado was applied to people in Spain who claimed special spiritual and exclusive enlightenment from within, communicated to them by a higher source. Numerous such groups had sprung up in Spain, France, and Italy during the fifteenth and sixteenth centuries. Their members were called Illuminati outside of Spain, and they enthusiastically advocated a pseudo-mysticism that ignored ecclesiastical doctrinal accuracy, church and papal authori-

living one, the one who merits the name that extinguishes all others. Whether one wants to call this experience mysticism or something else is irrelevant here: how something like that can be made even remotely clear and put into human words is for your theologians to figure out. Why such an experience does not preempt a relationship with Jesus, hence, with the church, I will address to some extent a little later.

But first: I have encountered God; I have experienced him. Even back then I was able to distinguish between God and the words, the images, the limited individual experiences that somehow point to God. This experience with God had, of course, its own story, which started off small and modest; I talked and wrote about it in a way that even I consider touchingly naïve now and that allows one to see what I meant to say only indirectly and as from afar. But the fact remains: beginning with Manresa I experienced increasingly and ever more distinctly the mysterious incomprehensibility of God. Even back then my friend Nadal[7] gave an account of it in his more philosophical way.

---

ty, and the rational framework of scholastic theology. Due to his mystical practices and teachings, Ignatius had become suspect of being one of them and had been arrested short-term in Spain by representatives of the Inquisition.

7 Jerónimo Nadal (1507–1580) had met Ignatius in 1526 at Alcalá and in 1532 in Paris when both were students at the universities, but was left with a negative impression of him. Ordained a priest in 1538 and graduating from the

God himself, truly, God himself I experienced, and not simply human words about him. It was he and the sovereign freedom that is his and can be experienced only at his initiative and not by the intersecting of finite realities and calculations about it. God himself I experienced, even though the "face-to-face" that I am experiencing now is something different and yet still the same, and I have no need to give theological lectures about this distinction. I say: that's how it was. And I would add: if you allowed your skepticism, driven by a sublime atheism regarding such a statement, to fully develop to its extreme, not only in clever theoretical speech but also in the bitterness of real life, you could have such an experience yourself. For then, there comes a moment when death presents itself (though one remains biologically alive) either as radical hope not dependent on anything apart from itself or as absolute despair, and it is at that moment that God offers himself. It is little wonder that I myself back then at Manresa stood on the

University of Paris, Nadal returned to his Majorca homeland, where he was studying Hebrew. In 1545, he was invited by a Majorcan priest to visit Rome and assist in preparing a general council of the church, later to be known as the Council of Trent. While in Rome, he visited the Jesuits, making the exercises and experiencing a conversion that led him to enter the Jesuit novitiate the same month. Nadal became one of Ignatius's closest associates, overseeing the founding of the first Jesuit colleges and helping promulgate the order's *Constitutions* to chapters in Portugal, Spain, France, Austria, the Netherlands, and Germany.

very threshold of suicide. While such an experience is the result of grace, it is also available in principle to all. Of precisely that I was certain.

Instructions on coming to such a personal experience

I did not consider the grace I experienced at Manresa and in later life all the way up to the solitude on my death bed, as a special privilege of a uniquely chosen person. That is the reason that I gave the exercises to whoever was open to such an offer of spiritual help. I gave the exercises even before I had studied your theology and managed (I'm laughing now) with considerable effort to earn the "magister" in Paris, even before I had obtained the ecclesial-sacramental privileges of my ordination to the priesthood. And why not? The retreat master who gives the exercises (as you would later come to call him) does not officially teach the word of the church with these basic instructions, despite their ecclesial nature, but merely offers assistance (provided he is capable) subtly and as from afar, so that God and the person can truly encounter each another in an immediate way. Even my first companions varied greatly in their giftedness for this task, and by the time I came to Paris I had lost every single one of those I had tried to win over through the exercises.[8] Once more:

8   While studying at Barcelona, Alcalá, and Salamanca.

Could the church of my time and can the atheism of yours really be taking for granted that something like that should exist, is permitted to exist, that the former age did not discard it as heretical subjectivism and that your age does not denounce it as an illusion and mere ideology?

In Paris, I had added to my exercises the rules for thinking with the church. I successfully fought my way through all the ecclesiastical legal trials that I was continually saddled with, and made my ministry and that of my companions subject to the immediate orders of the pope. I will have to say more about that later and in greater detail. But the fact remains: God can and wants to deal with his creature directly; and one can experience such dealings concretely. One can appropriate God's sovereign offer of freedom for one's own life, and such a step is no longer the result of objective grassroots calculations guided by the imperative of human reason, nor is it the result of philosophical, theological, or "existential" deliberations.

Ignatian spirituality

To me, this rather simple and yet enormous conviction (along with a few other things that I have yet to address) appears to be the essence of what you commonly call my spirituality. Does one look at this spirituality through the lens of the history of ecclesial piety, is it old or new in that regard, is it to be taken for granted or shocking? Does it mark the beginning of the "modern era" of the church, and is it perhaps more closely related to the original experiences of Luther and Descartes than you Jesuits have been willing to admit over the centuries? Is it something that will take a backseat again in the church of today and tomorrow, where one is almost incapable of bearing the enormous solitude before God and thus tries to flee into the community of church life, even though such a community should be made up of spiritual people, those who have encountered God, and not those who are using the church to be ultimately avoiding God and his sovereign incomprehensibility? Such questions, my friend, are no longer relevant to me, hence beg no answers. I am no prophet regarding the church's future developments. You yourself will have to ask these questions and find answers to them both by way of theological reasoning and historical decision-making.

Still, this remains: a person can experience God personally. And your pastoral care should always and at every stage keep this goal invariably in mind. In fact, you would be forgetting and even betraying my "spirituality" in your so-called pastoral care and your missionary efforts if you were to fill the barns of human awareness with your educated and modernized theology only, even if it were the choicest at that, which ultimately produces nothing but a miserable avalanche of words. You would also be betraying it if you were to train people only in how to become churched, making them enthusiastic subjects of the church as an institution; if you were to make out of them those who are obedient subjects of a distant God who is represented by ecclesiastical authority; if you were not helping people overcome all that, helping them to ultimately let go of all tangible assurances and individualistic insights for the sake of a confident letting-go into this final incomprehensibility that no longer has any paths, and if you did not manage to do so amidst the final, terrible impasses of life and the immeasurability of love and joy and, radically and ultimately so, by death (together with the god-forsaken, dying Jesus). Since all people are sinners and shortsighted, I may be permitted to say that not infrequently did you Jesuits throughout your history sin by oblivion and betrayal. Not infrequently did you defend the church as if she were the ultimate, but not as the very event where, when true to her own nature, people silently surrender to God and no longer want to know what exactly it is they are doing, only that it is God who is the incomprehensible mystery who can only by surrender become our goal and our blessedness.

I should state now more explicitly, especially for you subconsciously covert atheists of today, how one can encounter God directly all the way to the unfolding of an experience where one then meets God in all things and not just in the specifically "mystical" moments, and where everything, in light of him, becomes transparent without disappearing from view. Actually, I should say something about the circumstances that are especially conducive to such experiences if these experiences are to be made truly clear and that in your age do not necessarily have to be like the ones I sought to generate with the exercises—though I am convinced that these exercises can still be more successful, quite literally, even in your time than some fashionable "improvements" that you are practicing here and there. I should clarify that the awakening of such an experience with the divine is actually not an infusion of something not previously present in the person, but the explicit coming into one's own and the free acceptance of the human disposition that is always present, frequently buried and pushed aside, but inevitably there in what is called grace and in which God himself is concretely present.

Perhaps I need to tell you, odd as it may seem, that there is no reason for you to run as if parched to the Eastern springs of self-forgetfulness, as if we ourselves had run out of the springs of living water, while haughtily saying that only deep human wisdom could flow from these springs and not the true grace of God. But I cannot continue talking about this here. You have to think about it yourselves by probing and testing it. The true cost of the experience I am talking about is the heart, which surrenders in trusting hope to the kind of love that loves one's neighbor.

The religious institution and
the God experience from within

Once more, I want to clarify what I just said by an illustration. There is the soil of a heart. Should it be left a wasteland and a desert where the demons dwell, or should it be a fertile land that bears the fruits of eternity? It seems that the church has constructed immense and complicated irrigations systems in order to water the soil of this heart and make it fertile by her word, her sacraments, her institutions, and guidelines for living. Certainly, all these "irrigation systems," if one may be calling them that, are good and necessary, though the church may readily admit that the soil of a heart can bear the fruits of eternity even where the church's "irrigation systems" do not reach. Of course, this image is ambiguous. And the activities of the church in proclamation and sacrament have aspects and reasons and necessities that are not well illumined by it. Yet let us stick with this image. Here then is what I think: Besides these external waters, imported from outside as it were into the land of the soul in order to irrigate it—and now without image, such as by religious doctrines on the principles of God and his commandments, and beyond that by whatever merely points to God and to which belong also the church, scripture, sacraments, etc.— there exists a deep well on this land itself, so that from this source, once drilled, bubble up on the land itself the waters of the living spirit unto eternal life, just as it is written in the Gospel of John.[9] As already indicated, the image is skewed; there is no ultimate contradiction between one's own inner source and the "irrigation system" without. Naturally, these two realities are interdependent. Every external call in the name of God, to use another image, only wants to affirm the internal promise that God himself gives, and such a promise needs some earthly form, though such a form can be much more varied and modest than your former theologians permitted. And it is valid even if such a call from without consisted of a call to responsibility, to love and fidelity, to self-giving service on behalf of freedom and justice in society and if it should sound much more worldly than your theologians would like to hear.

And yet, I stubbornly insist again and again: such indoctrinations and imperatives from without, such pipelines of grace from outside are of use only if they meet with the ultimate grace from within. And this was my personal experience beginning with my very own and first exercises at Manresa, where the eyes of my spirit were opened and I could see everything as in God. This is the experience I wanted to convey to others by the giving of the exercises. It seems self-evident to me that such assistance in obtaining an immediate encounter with God (or should one say: the experience that people have always had and still do?) is especially important today because of the danger that all external

9   In reference to John 4:14.

theological indoctrinations and all moral imperatives are being swallowed up by the deathly silence that today's atheism generates, so people are unable to see that this terrible silence speaks yet again of God.

Once again and ever more: I am no longer able to give the exercises, so that my assurance that God can be encountered directly remains an empty promise. Do you now understand why I say that the main task around which everything should be revolving for you Jesuits is the giving of the exercises? Of course, I do not mean by that primarily the courses offered through the local parish office and given to many people at once, but the type of mystagogical help given to others that does not subdue the immediacy of God but allows it to be clearly experienced and accepted. That is not to say that every single one of you is able to give or should give the exercises that way; not every one of you ought to think he can. This is no denigration of all the other work in the fields of pastoral care, science, or socio-politics that you thought you needed to pursue in the course of your history. Rather, all these other activities should be seen by you as preparation for, or as consequence of, your ultimate task, which even in the future will remain yours: offering people assistance with an immediate God experience so they recognize that the incomprehensible mystery that we call God is near, can be addressed, and will gladly shelter us, provided we do not try to subdue this mystery but, instead, surrender to it without reserve. You should be testing all your activity repeatedly to see whether it serves this goal. If so, then let a biologist among you go so far as to examine the spiritual life of a cockroach.

God's leaning toward the world

When I say that God can be encountered directly even in your time as he could in mine, I mean by that truly God, the God of incomprehensibility, the unspeakable mystery, the darkness that becomes eternal light only to those who allow themselves to be unconditionally swallowed up by it, by the God who no longer has a name. But precisely this God, he and no other, was experienced by me as the God who comes down to us, who draws near us, by whose incomprehensible fire we are not consumed but, instead, become ourselves and remain everlasting. The unspeakable God gives himself to us; and in this act of giving in his inexplicability we become alive, we are being loved and become of eternal value; when we allow ourselves to be taken by him, we are not destroyed by him but receive ourselves back from him. The insignificant creature becomes eternally significant, unspeakably great and beautiful on account of God's gifting himself to it.

I realized that without God we would be erring about in the space of our freedom and our decisions, ever uncertain and ultimately ending up in desperate boredom because everything we had chosen was bound to be finite and to being replaced by something else finite, so that it all was the same. I realized that in the space of my freedom and its possibilities, the infinitely free God of all my possibilities had chosen to regard with special affection only one possibility over against the others, so that only one in contrast to the others remained that was transparent toward him and did not obstruct him but permitted one to love him by choosing it and it in him, thereby revealing itself as "the will of God."

When I placed the available possibilities and their potential outcomes before me in light of the impending free choice to be made, I discovered that one option clearly fitted into the wide freedom of God and remained transparent toward him, while the other did not, even though all options could be small signs of this infinite God which, each in its own way, derived from him. While difficult to make clear, this is approximately how I learned to distinguish—even within the area of the objectively and rationally possible and that which was permissible by social and ecclesiastical standards—between what held the incomprehensibility of the infinite God who wanted to be near me and what remained somewhat dark and non-transparent toward God, even if the latter had been tested and seemed to make more sense. It would be foolish to simply say that all that is true because it truly came from God must lead every person equally to God since it would render meaningless any decision in its inevitability and made in complete freedom.

But what I just said does not sufficiently describe this experience of God's "incarnation" in his creature, which does not become smaller as the creature draws nearer to God. As incomprehensible as it may seem, there is something like a joint human venture with God's descent into this finitude, which has now become benevolent because the person who happens to come directly before God experiences it with God. During this process, the one who is praying and acting must not lose focus of the nameless, incomprehensible, unmanageable, unpredictable God. And God must not become the sun that makes everything visible yet cannot be seen. Instead, God needs to remain immediate with what I would call a merciless clarity so that everything in its limitations and relativity is held in check.

But precisely this option that is favored through God's self-giving love, in contrast to the others, appears under this unfavorable light as that which is loved and preferred and chosen to exist among the numerous other options that remain empty. And this leaning of God toward the concrete, finite creature is experienced by the person standing in the non-directive light of God. The person is allowed and able to take seriously the finite, and it becomes to the person lovely, beautiful, of ultimate eternal value because God himself can and does work the incomprehensible miracle of his love by giving himself to the creature. With this participation in the turning of God toward the person and God's descent into finitude without thereby diminishing or burning up this finitude, the person can no longer remain the one whose most secret plight and pleasure it is to unmask the relativity and insignificance of everything and all, and the person can no longer remain the one who either idolizes something in creation or who (ultimately) destroys it. This experience of God's leaning toward what is not God and the realization that thereby the creature who is separate from God is also intertwined with him, is made at first wherever one experiences that something over against another is desired by God, just the way I indicated. But since this "other" toward which God leans is more specifically the person next to you and not a thing, the participation in God's inclination is what makes for a true love of neighbor. I will say something more about that later on. One's love of God may seem as if it cared little about the world but it is really a love of the world, also, because it loves the world along with God and thus allows for the world's unfolding toward eternity.

Participation in the Descent of God into the World

Of course these are only words about an experience, and they cannot generate the experience itself. The experience of this participation in God's inclination has to be made personally. Here, too, as in other instances, one cannot piece together the whole from previously separate parts; it has to be given as a whole and can

21

only then and there unfold in its unity and diversity and be incorporated into the freedom of the person in an increasingly unconditional way: one has to love one's neighbor in everyday life spontaneously as a matter of course and more and more so in unselfish and honest fashion. God in his sovereignty has to become ever more evident. The inseparable unity of love of God and love of neighbor and their mutual interrelatedness have to become ever more apparent to the person in his or her freedom. Since at first the love of neighbor appears as the more self-evident, even if it always risks deathly despair and disappointment over what is remiss in the lover or the beloved, one should have to start, now as then, with the resolve to do what is not self-evident, namely, to seek God directly and to make the exercises with that in mind. Making the exercises in this context has initially nothing to do with concrete retreat houses, classes organized through the parish office, elaborate catechesis, etc. At any rate, the love for God, not the love of a human theory about God, is the ultimate ground for a love toward one's neighbor, one that can be a necessity and yet retains its freedom.

Christian meditation as the experience of God's immediacy does not make the world disappear or disperse. Whether this is true also for your Eastern methods of meditation that are of such great appeal to you today, as if there were nothing comparable in the explicitly Christian realm, you will have to figure out for yourself. If it is, I am not opposed to your borrowing from the

East, for then even here God actively pours out his spirit over all flesh. If not, you had better be careful. At any rate, you should not succumb to the temptation today to assume that this silent and non-directive incomprehensibility that we call God could not and would not be allowed to turn to you of his own accord out of free love to make himself real, to anticipate your move, to empower you from your innermost center in which he resides, and to allow you to say "You" to him, the nameless one. Something like this is an incomprehensible mystery, blasting to pieces your entire system of metaphysics, and its possibility can be grasped only when its reality is courageously probed. It is the miracle that itself belongs to the inexpressibility of God which would be empty formality and yet again become subject to your metaphysics unless one had experienced it in the here and now as God's leaning toward us. You must be cautious not to assume that this "You" is only what precedes the descent into God's vast incomprehensibility; rather, it is its effect and results from one's own absolute surrender to God's leaning toward us, so that God is allowed to become even bigger than we previously thought, provided we see ourselves as utterly dependent and as if nothing before him.

Jesus

Now I will need to talk about Jesus. Did what I have said so far sound as if I had forgotten Jesus and his blessed name? I did not forget him, for he was already implicitly present in all I said, even though the words that are spoken among you have to follow a sequence and one cannot say everything at once. I am saying it now: Jesus. Based on your understanding of the "history of piety," you might say that the Jesus piety I tried to address in the exercises is only an echo of the Jesus piety common during the Middle Ages, beginning with Bernard of Clairvaux and on to Francis of Assisi, and that I merely inserted a few terms borrowed from a late-medieval feudalism that even back then was on the verge of vanishing.

I readily admit that one can find in my writings many instances of such a medieval Jesus piety. I gladly exempt you from the need to research the footprints on the Mount of Olives that the Lord supposedly left there when ascending to heaven. But why should I be perturbed when being charged with a lack of originality in this matter? Is this medieval Jesus piety outdated or is it a message that has yet to be understood today? Does it not contain the promise of fulfillment, a fulfillment that you yourselves are looking for with your modernized Jesus piety, which assumes that it can reach people only when one proclaims in a self-important and simplistic manner the death of God, rather than understanding that it is precisely in the person of Jesus that God communicates himself and promises himself?

In my days, it was no problem to find God in Jesus and Jesus in God, apart from the problem of actually practicing love and true discipleship. One could find God uniquely in him, the way he truly was, so that only love and not dissenting reason was in a position to declare in what way Jesus was to be imitated and followed. It was in him that one could talk of him and of the story of God, the eternal and incomprehensible one, without the need of dissecting this story into theory, but rather with a need of telling it over and over again so that it could continue. Since my conversion experience, I considered Jesus to be the very inclination of God toward the world and toward me, the inclination where the incomprehensibility of pure mystery was completely present and where the person could reach his or her complete fulfillment. I was never troubled by the specificity of Jesus, the necessity of having to look for him in the limited scope of his recorded actions and words in order to find in this small piece the eternal presence of the unspeakable mystery. Hence, the travel to Palestine was to me truly a travel into the pathless presence of God, and you, not I, are naïve and superficial when assuming that my longing for the Holy Land for nearly fifteen years was simply the obsession of a medieval person or something comparable to the longing for Mecca of a Muslim today. My longing for the Holy Land was a longing for Jesus, the concrete one, the one who is not simply an abstract idea.

There is no Christianity that can find the incomprehensible God apart from Jesus. God desired that innumerably many people would find him, provided they truly search for Jesus and that when falling into the deathly abyss, they do so together with Jesus in his own god-forsakenness, even though they may not be able to describe this fate of theirs by using his blessed name. God permitted such darkness in finitude and such guilt to exist in his world only because he could make them his own in Jesus. This is the Jesus I held in my thoughts, this is the Jesus I loved, and this is the Jesus I sought to follow. This is how I encountered God without making him out to be the phantom of mere non-committal speculation. For one can only overcome such speculation when throughout life one dies a concrete death. But a person has only died a good death when stalwartly accepting, like Jesus, one's own internal god-forsakenness; only that is ultimate pathless mysticism. I am aware that by saying this I have not explained the mysterious unity of history and God. But in Jesus, the crucified and risen one, the one who lets go of God and receives God, such unity is present in absolute form and can be accepted in faith, hope, and love.

Discipleship of Jesus

I have to say a little more about this Jesus and about Christian discipleship all the way up to the foolishly loving imitation of him. But even in that I do not claim originality since even here the old message is coming to meet you from a future where you have not yet arrived.

It is true that one has found Jesus completely, and with him God, only when one has died with him. But if one understands that this dying with him has to happen throughout one's own life, then certain idiosyncrasies of Jesus' life gain a terrifying meaning, even though they appear at first glance to be incidental and conditioned by the history and society of the time. I do not know whether the idiosyncrasies of Jesus' concrete, ordinary life that certainly held me in spell do make a clear and concrete impression on those who, either officially or anonymously, find God and are being saved. It does not seem that way. It seems as if there are many ways of following Jesus. It makes little sense to try and find a common denominator for all these different paths, to try and distill from these varied and concrete expressions of discipleship one unified picture of discipleship by saying that they are all one "in spirit." That may be true: of course there is one ultimate form of Christian discipleship since there is one God, one Jesus, one basic nature in humans, and one eternal life. But still, there are concrete expressions of this discipleship and they are different, they remain exceedingly different, and they even appear to threaten one another or to negate one another. Did Pope Innocent III[10] and Francis

10 Innocent III was pope between 1198 and 1216, which were years of profound change in both church and world. Under his reign, the pope obtained the role as ecclesiastical ruler of the world. Trained as a theologian and lawyer, Innocent believed that since things of the spirit took preeminence over

of Assisi[11] practice the same type of discipleship or was one so different from the other—and each of the two men had one—that only by a near desperate summons of love and patience did they manage to coexist with each other? Are there not different charisms, and is it truly possible to understand more than one or the other charism, the one that is one's own?

Whatever the case may be, I have chosen to follow

things of the body, and since the church ruled the spirit and earthly monarchs the body, earthly monarchs had to be subject in all things to the pope. In addition to his power politics, he waged a crusade, convened the Fourth Lateran Council in 1215 as one of the key councils in history, fought heresy through the work of smaller orders, and encouraged the founding of two new ones: the Dominicans and the Franciscans. In 1210, he gave verbal approval to Francis of Assisi's order, then through an indulgence in 1216. He also was the original impetus for Dominic's mission, which failed to be approved as an order by the 1215 Lateran Council, but was granted approval the following year by Honorius III, Innocent's successor.

11 Francis of Assisi (c. 1181–1226) was the son of a wealthy cloth merchant and spent his youth in extravagant living and war activities. A vision of Christ in 1206 caused him to change his lifestyle, devoting himself to a life of abject poverty and austerity, the care of the sick and the poor, and preaching. In 1215, the female Franciscan order of the Poor Clares was begun under the leadership of Clare of Assisi (1194–1253), who had been converted under Francis's preaching, and whose order practiced the same austerities of self-discipline with a commitment to absolute poverty.

the poor and humble Jesus. It is the poor and humble one and no another. Such a choice springs directly from a concrete love, is a calling that carries its own legitimacy; it is not something that may simply be imposed on all Christians or could be imposed on them with the clever explanation that it were a matter of spiritual poverty and humility, a matter of attitude. I make no claims to originality, and the saints in heaven do not compare themselves with one another but, apart from my visible lifestyle during the last years of being superior general of the order, I did as early as Manresa practice the kind of poverty in my life that was as radical as the one of Francis of Assisi, even though his and my time were quite different sociologically and economically speaking. By necessity, this difference also resulted in a difference of lifestyle between the two of us: In contrast to Francis, I wanted to study and had to,[12] so that the resulting differences would undoubtedly have been recognized and approved of by St. Bonaventure[13]

12 The early years of the Franciscan order were marked by the spiritual discipline of poverty in solidarity with the poor and the sick, with begging and works of mercy, and with preaching. Francis never was ordained to the priesthood, hence did not have a theological education. His own background and the ideals of his order left little room initially for academic studies and the reading or writing of books. At the dawn of the modern era, humanism had prompted the study of early writers, rhetoric, pursuits in the sciences, and higher learning.

13 Bonaventure (1221–1274) became a Franciscan at age 17

without being able to deny that I truly followed the poor Jesus. If you read my autobiography, you will see what I mean here.

Following the humble Jesus produced the spiritual and ecclesiastical lifestyle that was that of its own time and became irreconcilable with secular power positions, but, beyond that, also led to poverty in regard to ecclesiastical power, ecclesiastical benefices, and the honors of the episcopate. To put it differently if I may, I was dead serious about the "marginalization" of my existence both in secular and church life. This was not imposed on me from the outside.

Having been born into one of the best Basque families and having had connections with the elite of the world and the church of the time, I could have easily made "something of myself," and in doing so I could

and went on to study in Paris, where he subsequently taught between 1248 and 1255. After a year's hiatus that temporarily excluded members of mendicant orders from university life, Bonaventure received his doctorate in theology, with Thomas Aquinas, in 1557. The same year he was elected minister general of the order. In 1260, he promulgated a set of constitutions on the rule with lasting effects for the order, was appointed cardinal-bishop of Albano in 1273, and served on a council that sought to effect reunion of the Eastern churches with Rome. Considered one of the great minds of medieval times and later declared a doctor of the church, Bonaventure wrote numerous theological and spiritual books, biblical commentaries, and the official biography of St. Francis.

have easily said that through power and rank I was serving people, church, and God in a selfless and sacrificial way. I even could have convinced myself that I was able to do more by being in such secular and church-related hierarchical positions than by becoming a small, poor waif living on the margins of society and the church. The fact that by virtue of my founding an order and serving as its superior general I became somebody else again is another matter, and I must say something about that in a little bit. In short: I wanted to follow the poor and humble Jesus, that and nothing else. I wanted what was not at all a given, what cannot be derived from the "nature of Christendom," what neither then nor now was and is being practiced by the prelates of the church and by the better clergy in countries that still consider themselves the fortresses of Christendom. I wanted what was neither motivated by church ideology nor an urge to formulate a social critique, though it may be of importance to both of these areas. I wanted as a rule for my life whatever the foolish love of Jesus suggested to me without looking right or left, since I had been unable to find God, the eternal and incomprehensible one, apart from his unconditional reality and despite reality's limitations and causal nature. Included herein and not excluded is the fact that such social and ecclesiastical marginality became to me the deliberate practice of dying with Jesus, a death which is the judgment and the blessed fate of all people, even of those who cannot or prefer not to follow Jesus in this way.

Powerless service

See how in my own time I opposed the appointment of my followers to episcopal and similar church positions, and with success! The reason was not to prevent my group's best people being taken away from me. If a Jesuit becomes bishop or cardinal today, you do not find that unusual. In fact, it seems normal to you that this should happen because of certain periods in history where a Jesuit cardinal was almost a regular institution. Do you see how my and your mentalities differ? You will say: Times were different back then and such an appointment today no longer makes one a powerful man. That is not true! For one, even today's cardinals and bishops are people who are very much tempted by power. For another, you would still need to ask yourselves which places, offices, switchboards in today's church you would have to renounce in order to live in my spirit and serve people through the church without any "power" and only in the sole trust in the power of the spirit and the foolishness of Christ.

Of course you are welcome to become a bishop like Hélder Câmara,[14] who risks everything for the poor. But

14 Hélder Câmara (1909–1999) was archbishop of Olinda and Recife, the poorest and least developed region of Brazil. Ordained to the priesthood in 1931, he was named bishop in 1952. Around that time, he was instrumental in founding the National Bishops Conference of Brazilian Bishops, the first of such a body in Latin America, for which he served as

think about where today's "bishops' seats" are, though they may be called by a different name. You should not be sitting on them, even though it is undeniable that these chairs are indispensable in the church. I am conscious of the problem that is at the root of this: How can a charismatic community committed to the radical discipleship of Jesus be also an ecclesiastical institutionalized order? Of course I was happy when the order was officially recognized by the popes during my lifetime. And you will need to continue trying to embody this amazing identity. There will never be a perfect balance. But keep trying, nonetheless! One of the two alone is not enough. Only both together do sufficiently make for the cross.

When I speak about the "poor" and "humble" Jesus

secretary for twelve years. Under his leadership, the conference became an advocate for the poor, defender of human rights, and grassroots communities and education. By empowering the poor, he wanted to make them agents of transformation. When made archbishop in 1964, he moved from the palace to a humble dwelling, encouraged the training of lay catechists, gave church land to provide a settlement for the landless, took seminarians out of the seminary to live in small base communities, and opened a seminary for seminarians and lay people, including women. During the Second Vatican Council (1962–1965), Câmara was regarded as one of the most influential figures on the progressive wing of the Council and soon came to be seen as an outspoken champion of the oppressed and poor throughout the world.

whom I wanted to follow, then you will need to translate these words in theory and practice to truly understand them. You will need to ask: What does it mean to be "poor and humble" today? When one becomes a Jesuit today, it is possible that one turns rather quickly and easily into a devout person and a priest, but not necessarily into a poor and humble individual. You yourselves will need to find out what the concrete translation of these words is in the modern-day world. Perhaps it means that the individual members will have to find out first before the translation can become clear to the order as a whole. But for heaven's sake, do not flee into mere good intentions, which even the prelates of the church may have. Translating poverty and humility for today will mean that these terms will carry a critical socio-political sting in secular society and in the church, a dangerous remembering of Jesus and a threat to business as usual in the church's institutions. Otherwise, the translation is no good. But that is merely a criterion to you and not the underlying motivation. The motivation is Jesus, the one dying unto death, he and not the socio-political impulse. He alone can preserve you from the fascination with power, present in the church in a thousand different facets, both now and in the future; he alone it is who will be able to protect you from the all-too-plausible thought that ultimately one can serve people only by having power; he alone can make comprehensible and bearable to you the holy cross of his powerlessness.

Fruitful and failed discipleship

I can no longer get around saying something about how my lifestyle of trying to follow the poor and humble Jesus has influenced the story of the order. When considering this story from the perspective of God's eternity, embraced by the loving will of God, apart from which all that was and is would be meaningless, one can look at such a story in a relaxed and mild manner and still find its particular meaning and place. One is no longer presented with the dilemma of regarding such a story simply as one's own history of influence or of viewing it as the chronicle of the sons' departing from the spirit of the father. That said and put before you as Jesuits, I will have to say that in this point at least and for right now, the order has not truly followed me. Of course, there were those among you who truly practiced poverty and humility and who did not just have good intentions. There was, for example, Peter Claver,[15] the

15 Peter Claver (1580–1654) was born in Verdu, near Barcelona, where he attended the university and joined the Jesuits in 1600. Following further studies, he was a missionary to New Grenada in 1610 and was ordained in Cartagena, in present-day Colombia, in 1615. The city was a hub of slave trade. Trying to alleviate the horrible conditions of the slaves, he worked in the yards where the slaves were penned after being disembarked from the ship from West Africa, ministering to them with food and medicine, teaching them the catechism, and baptizing them. He is reported to have made some three hundred thousand con-

slave of slaves in Latin America; Francis Regis,[16] who shared the fate of his poor farmers; Friedrich von Spee,[17] who stood by the so-called witches amidst threats to his life and exclusion from the order; the many Jesuits who in past centuries traveled aboard horrible ships to Eastern Asia only to be killed there, and many, many others, and, in moving all the way to the

verts during the forty years of his ministry among the slaves. He also lobbied on behalf of the slaves with the slave owners and visited plantations around the city, usually lodging in the slaves quarters himself.

16 John Francis Regis (1597–1640) was born in Fontcouverte, France, the son of a rich merchant. He studied at a Jesuit college and joined the Jesuits in 1615. Ordained in 1631, he was assigned to do missionary work in southwestern France and became known for his ability to relate to the local farming community and the unlettered through his preaching, teaching, and hearing confessions. Thousands were converted to the faith by him and his preaching drew large crowds.

17 Friedrich von Spee (1591–1635) was born in Kaiserwerth, Germany, and studied in Cologne. In 1610, he joined the Jesuits and was ordained in 1622. The following year, he became a professor of moral theology in Paderborn and taught subsequently in Cologne and Trier. He wrote hymns that influenced the Baroque era. His principal treatise, *Cautio Criminalis*, was published in 1631 and called for the immediate abolition of trials for witchcraft. It described abuses, such as the use of the rack, argued against measures of violence, and demanded reform. His writings had the result that witch-burning was abolished in a number of cities in Germany, such as Mainz, and they paved the way to its gradual suppression.

present, also your friend Alfred Delp,[18] who before being hanged in Berlin in 1945 signed with bound hands the papers for final vows in the order. All these and others were most certainly disciples of the poor and humble Jesus, and they demonstrated the spirit I had taught them through the order.

But what about the order itself? You know that for weeks I prayed over and wrestled with the seemingly minor details regarding the order's vow of poverty;[19]

18 Alfred Delp (1907–1945) was born in Mannheim, Germany, and became a Jesuit in 1926. During World War II he joined an anti-Nazi group for which he was arrested in 1944. Confined to a dark cell and held in chains, Delp wrote a series of Advent and Christmas mediations, conscious that every day might be his last. The writings show how a person living in the presence of God can gain a sense of freedom that outer circumstances are powerless to overcome. Shortly after signing his final papers and taking solemn vows as a Jesuit, Delp was hanged in the Plötzensee prison camp in 1945. One of his teachers and friends had been Karl Rahner, S.J.

19 Ignatius had struggled with the degree of poverty that the Jesuits were to practice. Did the fixed income resulting from the order's administration of a parish and providing it with pastoral services represent a break with the vow of poverty? Ignatius feared that it did. Either late in January or early February of 1544, he decided to reexamine before God the pros and cons of accepting such income in what is known as his Deliberation on Poverty. The document illustrates Ignatius's own process of discernment in coming to reach a decision, a process in which he sought to instruct others by

this was to ensure that certain rules preserved the spirit of the poor and humble Jesus in the order, details you would have settled, no doubt, in a matter of hours by sober, rational discussion. When viewed as a whole in a sober and honest manner, you are aware that I did not succeed, as little as did Francis (and the Franciscans may forgive me here) in trying to preserve for the order the concrete discipleship of the truly poor Jesus.

Perhaps it is impossible to safeguard the spirit of an order through regulations. They either kill the spirit they seek to preserve or invariably allow for so much freedom that the space becomes occupied by a different spirit while the letter of the law stays intact. Is it really possible for a larger group to practice such a lifestyle without major concessions? Perhaps I overstepped the critical limits when in 1540 I and my companions, who were guided by my spirit, converted this charismatic circle, as you would call it today, into an ecclesiastically approved order. Given that by doing so, and in no other way, the ultimate impulses of the spirit of God continued to be at work throughout the centuries, should we really have refrained? Is not part of this spirit also to calmly and humbly renounce the expectation of purity and complete adherence to "ideals," this spirit that brings the history of the church and the world a little closer to God? In a world where the spirit always needs

his exercises and which, in his case, took him more than five weeks to complete.

to be embodied socially, hence is always threatened with extinction, should it be surprising that the order has become a place of economic security and, to say the least, ecclesiastical prestige for its members, even though the individual lives in an economically modest fashion and it is rare that one (rarer than in comparable circumstances) becomes a bishop or cardinal or another powerful lord in the church? Is all of this to be taken for granted or is it tragic?

Will the force of the past, especially on this question, also determine the future of the Jesuits? As an order, could they not become economically poor in a concrete manner in the future, regardless of individual preference, and become like the truly poor and be living from one handout to the next, yet accepting it gladly, without fail, together with the poor Jesus, and could this then also be of socio-critical relevance (as a consequence and not as the motive)? Could Jesuits suddenly live in a completely different and new way for reasons I cannot foresee at this point, hence live as the marginalized in ecclesiological society who are at a healthy, charismatic distance from hierarchy, which they will, of course, always respect? Did not Johann Baptist Metz[20]

20 Johann Baptist Metz (1928–) was born in Auerbach, Germany, and studied theology in Bamberg, Innsbruck, and Munich. He received his doctorate in 1952 and was ordained a priest in 1954. From 1963 to 1993, he was professor of fundamental theology in Münster and served for another four years as visiting professor in Vienna. A former

tell you recently something about that which should give you pause? All these are questions already answered in my eternity, but the answers to them for you can only emerge from history itself, and they cannot be translated into your time by premature words from my end.

At any rate, you Jesuits have the responsibility to show courage about the future because Jesus presents a legitimate lifestyle for the future by his actual life and death. You will have to search for what this lifestyle is to look like presently so it can be a true discipleship of the poor and humble Jesus tomorrow. I have been continually talking about the "poor" and "humble" Jesus

> student and close associate of Rahner's, Metz can be seen as the founder of a new type of political theology grounded in concrete history, as contrasted with Rahner's more transcendental approach that seemingly eschewed concrete historical and political events. Metz was also influenced by the Frankfurt School of social philosophy and progressive Catholicism and he, in turn, had a critical influence on liberation theology in Latin America. Metz's theology calls for a remembrance of and identification with those who are suffering. By ever keeping alive the question of theodicy and the remembrance of and identification with Jesus' passion as a *memoria passionis*, Metz believes that one can contribute to making the world a more humane place in the certain hope and anticipation of God's eschatological fulfillment. Rahner is referrring here to Metz's book *Zeit der Orden? Zur Mystik und Politik der Nachfolge* ("time for religious orders? On mysticism and the politics of discipleship"), published by Herder in 1977.

in the language of my time. Therefore, I will need to say it again: You may need to translate these words into different ones in order to understand and live them, so they are not an escape into purely good intentions or into a merely privatized professional asceticism. That certainly was more or less your tendency in the last one and a half centuries, where you failed to recognize sufficiently your social responsibility in regard to justice in the world, as little as did the church, despite some occasionally praiseworthy encyclicals.

Loyalty to the church

Now, I will have to say something about my devotion to the church and its significance to you at the present. Everybody expects hearing about that from me and rightfully so. As far as the objective meaning goes of the various things I will address, I should be very brief. Since God, Jesus, his discipleship, and the church are, despite their interrelatedness, quite different matters and hence have different meanings, I am not only entitled but obligated for all time and eternity to differentiate among these realities in all their significance and relevance. I am emphatically called a man of the church. Marcuse[21] calls me a soldier of the church. I am in no

21 Herbert Marcuse (1898–1979) was born in Berlin and studied philosophy at Freiburg. He earned a Ph.D. in 1922, worked in publishing, and returned to Freiburg in 1929 for

way embarrassed by my loyalty to the church. After my conversion, I wanted to serve the church with my entire life, even though such service is ultimately directed toward God and people and not toward a self-serving institution. The church has an eternal dimension because it is the community of people that believes, hopes, journeys, and loves God and others, of people who are filled with God's spirit. But I understand, of course, that the church is also the sociologically framed, concrete church in this history, the church of institutions, of the human word, of tangible sacraments, of bishops, of the Roman pope, of the hierarchical Roman Catholic Church. By calling me a man of the church, and I readily accept that, one has in mind the church in its tangible and harsh institutionalization, the "official church," which is what you tend to call it today in a tone that does not betray much enthusiasm. Yes, I was the man of that church and I wanted it to be, and I never felt that it conflicted with the radical immediacy of my conscience and my mystical experience.

further studies. His habilitation thesis was rejected by Martin Heidegger, but published in 1932 as *Hegel's Ontology and Theory of Historicity*. As a Jew, he found his academic career blocked by the rise of the Third Reich, so he left Germany in 1933, going first to Switzerland, then to the United States, where he became a citizen in 1940. Marcuse taught philosophy and politics at Columbia, Harvard, and San Diego universities and remained throughout his life a representative member of the Frankfurt School.

But my loyalty to the official church is completely misunderstood when interpreted as the egotistical, fanatic ideological, limiting love of power that seeks victory while ignoring the conscience, or, as identification with a "system" that is incapable of pointing beyond itself. Since we human beings tend to be short-sighted and sinful in life, I admit to having paid occasional tribute out of a false sense of loyalty and, should you be so inclined, you are welcome to scrutinize my life in factual and sober ways regarding this matter. But one thing is certain: overall, my loyalty to the church was only an expression, and an indispensable one at that, of my intention to "help souls," an intention that can become reality only to the extent that these "souls" are growing in faith, hope, love, and closeness to God.

All love for the official church would be idol worship, participation in the horrible egotism of a system concerned only with itself, unless it were guided by this intention and framed by it. But this also means, and the story of my mystical path gives testimony to that, that the love for this church, as unconditional as it may be, cannot be first and foremost in my life but has to be a *consequence* and the *result of* one's closeness to God, so that it receives from one's closeness to God both its meaning and its limitations and its distinct traits. To put it differently: I loved the church for its historic participation in God's inclination toward the concrete body of his son. And in this mystical union of God and the church, despite their radical difference, the church was and remained to me transparent toward God and the concrete place of this my inexpressible relationship with the eternal mystery. This is the source of my church loyalty, of my practice of the sacramental life, of my fidelity to the papacy, of the ecclesial nature of my calling to help souls. When my church loyalty is placed properly in the overall framework of my spiritual life, then even a critical stance toward the official church appears once again as an expression of loyalty to the church. Christians can maintain such a critical stance, since they are not simply identical with their church in all its external institutionalized forms but they stand in direct relationship with God and his gracious inspiration, an inspiration that sustains Christians in the church and is part of the church as the community of grace. This inspiration is not simply mediated through the church apparatus and can be something that the official church and its prelates must learn to pay attention to, unless the church prefers to become guilty of rejecting such movements of the spirit for the sole reason that they lack official approval.

Such a critical stance toward the church is, from the church's perspective, once more an example of church loyalty. After all, even as an organization the church remains ultimately open and subject to the spirit of God due to God's inclination toward the church, a spirit that is always more than institution, law, tradition of the letter, etc. Naturally, this relationship between spirit and institution has not immediately eliminated concrete conflicts between spirit-motivated Christians and church officials. Such conflicts will continue to flare up in ever new and surprising forms, so that one does not have ready recipes and institutional mechanisms for their resolution. In the final analysis, a Christian can become convinced only by faith that an absolute conflict need not exist inevitably and for all times between spirit and the institutionalized church. Christians can only humbly hope that God's providence will not lead them into a situation where an absolute pronouncement of the office and an absolute pronouncement of their conscience can no longer be reconciled and equally embraced. At any rate, partial and temporary conflicts in the church are part of the church's nature, and I have no need to suggest concrete recipes for their resolution. It is also true that the literal carrying out of an order from above is not the first and foremost criterion for church loyalty and obedience, just as I myself as the superior general of the order did not lead that way. If it were the first and foremost criterion, there could be no conflicts in the church. They exist, however, and they exist with and among the saints, beginning with Peter and Paul, hence, they are allowed to exist.

Even in the church, there is no law that says that the convictions and decisions of Christians and of the church's office-holders need to blend neatly and without friction. The church is a church of the spirit of the infinite and incomprehensible God, whose blessed unity can be mirrored in this world only in a broken fashion and in diverse fragments and whose ultimate appeased unity is only God himself and nothing else.

Do not think for one moment that my loyalty to the church spared me the experience of conflicts or that I downplayed them by a false church loyalty. I was no janissary[22] of the church or the pope. I had conflicts with office-holders in the church at Alcalá, Salamanca, Paris, Venice, Rome. On church orders, I was imprisoned for weeks both at Alcalá and Salamanca; even when already in Rome, I had to expend a lot of time and effort to deal with all this trouble and defend my loyalty to the church. When at La Storta[23] the Eternal Father promised to show me mercy in Rome, I envisioned as one possibility of receiving such "mercy" my crucifixion in papal Rome. All the bones in my body were shaking

22 Janissaries were an elite group of soldiers in the Ottoman army and directly responsible to the sultan as commander in chief. This group existed from the fourteenth to the nineteenth centuries in the Ottoman Empire, and the sultan himself would wear their uniform when visiting the camp. Janissaries trained under strict discipline with hard labor and under nearly monastic conditions in schools. They were expected to remain celibate for life, be good Muslims, and refrain from engaging in any other activities or trades apart from defending and advancing the expansion of the empire.

23 La Storta was only a few miles from Rome, and Ignatius received there a vision that was important to him and the future orientation of his spirituality as well as that of the order.

when Paul IV[24] was elected pope; and this same pope sent his police to serve me with a search warrant of our quarters when I already was the superior general of an order that had papal approval. Even as I lay on my death bed, I desired to have his blessing so that while I lay dying without even receiving the sacraments, I would yet again make a modest, polite gesture toward him. But by the time Polanco brought me this blessing, I had already died, and the news of this death of mine did not produce a particularly kind response from the pope. In short, I was and continued to be loyal to the church and the pope, even though I was persecuted and imprisoned by men of the church who carried official authority.

You will remember that, all in all, this unity of

24 Paul IV (1476–1559) was pope from 1555 to 1559 and known for his harsh and imperialistic manner that completely ignored the principles of the Council of Trent. Born Gianpietro Carafa into a Neopolitan aristocratic family, he was a fierce defender of the true faith and advocate of the Inquisition. During his papacy, he sentenced to the galleys monks whom the police found absent from their monasteries, he drove bishops from Rome back to their sees, and in 1559 issued the first Index of Forbidden Books under the supervision of the Congregation of the Inquisition. As a Neapolitan, he deeply resented Spanish control of southern Italy, which may explain in part his attitude toward the Jesuits and their founder, a Spaniard. When Paul IV died, the Roman populace destroyed in a riot his statues and the buildings of the Inquisition.

obedient service and critical distancing from the office of the church was always accompanied by such conflicts. And never was there one perennially valid and all-encompassing rule in history because this unity had to be newly created at any given time and, happily, it was created again and again. One has to look closely in order to discover in the order's history what counts as loyalty to the church and the papacy and what as criticism. A devout Pius V meddled with the order without any understanding whatsoever of its true nature.[25] In the so-called dispute on grace, the order and its theology were put on trial in Rome and only barely could avert a guilty verdict. The order had to fight for its moral theology against an alliance forged between Innocent XI and its own superior general, Gonzalez. In the seventeenth and eighteenth centuries, you lost the dispute over rites with the popes, who were more enamored with orthodox caution than innovative courage. The suppression of the order in 1773 by Clement XIV, with the rather shabby brief of suppression and the undignified incarceration of the superior general, Ricci,[26] by the pope, against whom Amnesty

25 Pius V had tried to impose on the Jesuits the monastic choral or communal liturgy of the hours, as practiced in the early Western monastic tradition of the Benedictines; also, he demanded that Jesuits not be ordained to the priesthood until they had professed final vows—a process that could take a decade or more.

26 Lorenzo Ricci was superior general from 1758 until the order's suppression in 1773, which was aimed at its com-

International would be mobilized today, was carried out under pressure from the Bourbons, whom the Revolution scattered shortly thereafter and who could certainly have been met with a little more resistance. This was no heroic stroke of papal wisdom and courage, no matter how clever the explanations are that historians might give. And blessed Pius X was intent on removing the superior general Wernz on account of being insufficiently integrationalist.[27]

One could certainly recount many more such and similar examples of a critical distancing between the official church and the order. Better yet would be if one could say that the order's renunciation of such honored offices as that of bishop and cardinal—hence a concrete distancing from the offices in the church (even though one affirms and respects them) would make such conflicts self-explanatory. However, the reality is that other

plete extinction. In 1770, the Society had 42 provinces, 669 colleges and seminaries, and about 23,000 members worldwide. Ricci himself had founded the Bavarian province of the order in 1770. He had to witness the slow death of the Society, where within two years the Portuguese, Brazilian, and East Indian provinces and missions were destroyed. Thousands of Jesuits were either killed or imprisoned. Ricci was imprisoned at the Castel San Angelo and tortured to death, dying in 1775.

27 Pius X (1835–1914) had condemned modernism as a heresy and demanded of every priest an oath against it, thereby impugning the orthodoxy of a number of eminent Catholic scholars, many of them Jesuits.

institutionalized joint ventures between the order and the office existed, so that the true purpose of renouncing such ecclesiastical honors would have been partially undermined. This is not to say that in the course of the long history of my order there were no instances where office and order identified with one another, though a critical distancing and a legitimate resistance would have been called for at the time. Of course, throughout its history the order has also been guilty repeatedly of defending the institutional church with its short-sightedness and sluggish inflexibility in such areas as theology, pastoral care, or law and of going against the spirit of the church. But fundamentally the fact remains that unconditional loyalty to the church and critical distancing from it in a spiritual sense are truly possible for me and my followers and have the sure right to exist based on the church's true nature. Therefore, you need not be embarrassed when a pope like Paul VI was not very happy with your 32nd General Congregation. It was much worse at the time of Pius V and Sixtus V, who both wanted to impose on you painful changes in your constitution.[28] I shall not talk about certain of your members who are surely odd characters and make one wonder why they remain Jesuits. As a whole, though,

28 Pius V had wanted to force Jesuits to keep the monastic hours of prayer and chant; Sixtus V insisted that the name of the order, Society of Jesus, needed changing, among other things in the constitution. Both popes died shortly before these changes could be fully implemented.

you are still loyal to the church and the papacy the same way I was, and such loyalty inevitably carries conflicts with it.

Jesuit obedience

In conjunction with the topic of church loyalty, it may be appropriate now to say something about the so-called "Jesuit obedience." On this topic, which is part of the history of piety, I do not claim much originality either, though such obedience has inevitably more weight in an active order with a common mission than in an abbey of contemplatives. This is true all the more when a worldwide order has a central place of governance and thus the relationship among individual members cannot be regulated on the basis of personal acquaintance and friendship. In essence, I still adhere to my teaching and practice on this point. The will to obedience, the determination to make oneself available to the joint mission of many and to voluntarily seek to fit in and submit to the community, is not an attitude to be ashamed of, even today. Decisions that need to be made in and for the sake of the community and that become binding for the individual cannot always be deliberated at length, discussed, or postponed until every single member has come to realize the practical correctness of such a decision. A "democratic" process of decision-making may be a good thing and may even be feasible in smaller groups. But it is utopia to assume that this is always possible when a decision is needed.

In the case of such decisions, which nearly always are to some degree questions of preference, one should not think that submitting to them despite personal disagreement with them is an injury to one's dignity. The underlying presupposition is, of course, that one affirms the community's unity and wants to serve a common cause, that one has this indifference, this detachment toward the individual possibilities of life and action, this willingness to practice self-critique by not taking oneself too seriously, all of which is being taught by the exercises and makes for the basis of your spirituality.

I certainly do not want to talk about obedience as being part of Christian discipleship. However, I am not so "democratic" in my teaching on obedience as to think that a binding decision is always more true and acceptable when made collectively as opposed to being made by an individual, even when either decision should run counter to the preference of the person affected by it. Both ways of decision-making have their advantages and disadvantages. A collective decision-making process is not necessarily more transparent, and one often is at a loss of knowing who to hold responsible for it. Even in today's secular world, a "democratic centralism" is not always viewed as outdated. In my order, too, the highest decision-making body is a parliament elected from below (in contrast to how the church is constituted), called the general congregation. The superior general is responsible to this body, even though he has far-ranging executive powers. Have you ever noticed that the constitution of your order is quite different from and more democratic than the papacy on which hinges the constitution of the larger church, the very papacy which you have been defending so decisively over the course of your order's history? In light of your democratic constitution and apart from other things, have you ever considered how incorrect it is to call the head of your order the "black pope"?

In addition, Jesuit obedience is embedded in the context of brotherly community. Just because this community is sober and practical and asks members not to expect a warm "nest" does not make it a false and artificial community. You might also want to demythologize a little the traditional teaching on obedience, despite its unconditional nature, and along with it what our dear Polanco wrote on my behalf in the famous letter on obedience.[29] Not everything in it is eternal truth. One should even expect that a superior today giving an order in good

29 Ignatius's *Letter on Obedience* was written to the Jesuits in Portugal on March 26, 1553. It was in response to the conduct of certain Portuguese Jesuits, whose lack of proper training brought them into conflict with superiors and had caused problems. At issue was up to which point to carry out obedience to one's superiors. By the time the situation was brought under control, more than a hundred members had left the order in Portugal or had been dismissed. Among the main factors that helped resolve the conflict was Ignatius's letter.

faith will occasionally hear from his "subordinate" a modest, yet unmistakable "no" because the latter cannot reconcile the order's content with his conscience.

Anyone willing to be "indifferent," to take a hard look at self, to be ready for quiet service for a common cause, to show a little humor and some patience besides with all the foolishness and deficiency of earthly affairs, should have no real problem today with obedience in the order. It even seems to me that the typical middle-class father of a family or a public employee has fewer freedoms in secular society than you do in the order. Regardless of the silly words in the letter on obedience, you are not expected to practice obedience in corpse-like fashion. But you ought to be people who are unselfish, sober, and willing to serve. There is such a thing as a "mysticism of service." But I do not want to address that here. Certainly, one will also need to demythologize "obedience" in regard to secular and state authority today. In the course of your history, you were too often devout "subjects" of secular establish-ments, even if, according to the theories of your great theologians of the Baroque era, you should not have had to be. In the eighteenth century, why did you not forcefully defend together with your Indians the holy experiment of the reductions[30] against the horrible

30 The Jesuit reductions were part of a missionary strategy that involved gathering the often nomadic people of South America into larger communities so they could be better evangelized and instructed in the Christian faith. Used main-

colonialism of Europe? Did you really have to let yourselves be pushed out of Latin America in the name of devout obedience?

Higher learning and the order

I am tempted to say something about the history of theology in my order, even if only something small can be deduced from it that may point to its future. But I can make only a few comments, though this history is by no means unimportant. The idea of probabilism that your moral theologians so strongly endorsed was quite remarkable for its time in that it defended a person's right to freedom of conscience. Today, one would have to call this idea by a different name.

> ly during the seventeenth and eighteenth centuries in what is today Paraguay, Brazil, Uruguay, and Mexico, reductions did not impose a European way of life but sought to teach the Christian faith and foster economic autonomy. Many of these reductions achieved a high degree of autonomy within the colonial empires, thus becoming self-sustaining and raising economic and living standards for its residents. When their existence was threatened by the incursions of the slave trade, the Jesuits helped build up militias of Indians to fight effectively against the colonists. The resistance of the Jesuit reductions to the slave trade and colonial interests as well as the communities' high degree of economic success are often cited as reasons for the Jesuits' expulsion from the Americas in 1767.

To be sure, you were humanists with a modern way of thinking in your theology, you regarded human beings and their essential "nature" with modern-day optimism, and you drew subsequent conclusions that informed your missionary activities in China and India, though Rome refused to recognize them. Whether intended or not, all of this was prelude to a theological anthropology that is necessary in a church that wants to be a church to the entire world and to all cultures and that refrains from selling European Christianity as an export article to the rest of the world. But the mistake with your optimistic anthropological approach from below was that you allowed a great many of your theologians to go against the basic presupposition of my exercises and to place divine grace beyond the reach of human awareness since you were convinced that this grace could not be personally known unless conveyed by means of external ecclesiastical indoctrination.

History confirms that your theology contributed to the type of faith development in the church that became concrete with Vatican I. This means that your theology today is obligated to develop further the approaches to the church's constitution made evident with Vatican II. You must remain loyal to the papacy in your theology (and in your practice) since that is a big part of your heritage. But since the papacy in its concrete expression will continue to be subject to historical changes, your theology and your church law should primarily serve the papacy of the future to be of help, rather than hindrance, in regard to Christian unity. Moreover, go on studying Marx, Freud, and Einstein; try to develop a theology that will find a hearing among people today and that can reach their hearts. But the starting and end point of your theology, which can be a truly systematic theology even today, remains Jesus Christ, the crucified and risen one, who is the promise of the incomprehensible God to the world and not a spiritual trend that is in one day and out the next.

Your theology has often been criticized for being plainly elitist. This is certainly and to some extent true. But if God is the "ever greater God" who can burst any system by which humans seek to subdue and rule reality, then your eclectic attitude can also mean that humans are pushed to their limits by the truth of God and are willing to accept their limitations. Ultimately, no system exists that would allow one to start at one place, the place where one stands, in order to capture all of reality. Your theology should not operate on the basis of cheap compromise and the absence of reason. Even in theology, you are pilgrims who by their repeated exodus are always in search of the eternal homeland of truth.

The order's possibilities for change

I have yet to say something about me and the order's potential impact on tomorrow, at least the impact I hope will occur, and that from quite a different perspective. From a historical point of view, the Society of Jesus is regarded as an order of schools, of theological education, of book publishing, and of influence on the mass media. All of this may be well and good and may correspond with the image that the order has projected during its four-hundred-year existence. I have already said that it is to be rightfully expected that the history of the sons is not simply a repetition of the lives of their fathers. I have already said that I am not sitting in judgment of the order's history. But that said, I still want to ask what this means to you and your future: What concretely does this history have to do with my lifestyle, the one I led especially from the time of my "Urchurch," as I used to call my time at Manresa, until up to the first years after I had settled in Rome, prior to my being absorbed with the work on the order's constitution, the management of the order, and my illness? After all, I and my first companions were no scholars and did not want to be, even if Francis Xavier[31] could

31 Francis Xavier (1506–1552) was born in the castle of Xavier, near Pamplona in the Basque region of Spain. He studied in Paris, where he met Ignatius, and earned his degree in 1528. He was one of the six founding members of the Society of Jesus. In 1540, he and Simon Rodriguez were sent to the East Indies as the first Jesuit missionaries. For the rest of his life, Francis traveled widely, serving in India, Malacca, the regions near New Guinea and the Philippines, and in Japan, preaching, teaching, baptizing, and making converts in the thousands while living in their midst.

have easily been one and Laínez[32] was an extremely bright theologian who made a deep impression at the Council of Trent. Of course: If one longs to serve God for the sake of people with all the radical freedom of the spirit and without restraint, where nothing is ultimately set beforehand and one is ready for anything, then one may be eventually obliged, provided one is capable and the situation demands it, to do theology, to write books, to become perhaps even a confessor at the royal court, to write letters to princes and prelates, and whatever else there is that should prominently come to define the history of the order for centuries. But during the decisive years we were quite different and the later development of the order would not mirror us properly.

We were true paupers and wanted to be like that. On our travels through France and Italy, we sought refuge in the dirty alms houses of the time. We cared for the sick in hospitals, such as the two hospitals in Venice for the incurables struck with syphilis, and this

32 Diego Laínez (1512–1565) was born in the Castile region of Spain and was of Jewish ancestry. He graduated from the university at Alcalá and continued studies in Paris, where he met Ignatius. One of the six original founders of the order, Laínez taught scholastic theology for years, engaged in various missions, including in Germany, and became one of the papal advisors during the Council of Trent, especially at its last session in 1562–1563. Upon Ignatius's death in 1556, he acted as vicar general of the order and was elected superior general two years later by the general congregation.

was quite different from the demands that are being made today on the staff in modern clinics. We preached in the streets, if necessary in a mixture of Spanish, Italian, and French. We lived the life of beggars. Teaching the catechism to small, lice-ridden children was faith turned to practice and not just a pious reminiscence, as in today's formulas spoken during the profession of vows.

While I took the initiative for the founding of the Gregoriana[33] and the Germanicum,[34] I also founded the

33 Ignatius founded this school in 1551 with the financial help of the viceroy of Catalonia, Francis Borgia, who later became a Jesuit. The school was first called the Collegio Romano or Roman College and it is considered the first Jesuit university. Today the college is the Pontifical Gregorian University, known as the Gregorianum, with one of the largest theology departments in the world, and a student body of about 1,300 from more than 130 countries, mostly candidates for the priesthood, priests, and members of religious orders.

34 The Germanicum was founded by Ignatius in 1552 as a seminary for German-speaking priests and seminarians in Rome due to the threat to the Catholic faith by the Protestant Reformation in German-speaking countries. In 1580, the seminary merged with the Collegium Hungaricum, founded in 1578, to become the Collegium Germanicum et Hungaricum for short. During World War I, the college's members had to move to the Collegium Canisianum in Innsbruck from 1915 to 1919. Since 1989, with the fall of the Soviet Union, the Collegium's international character in its student body has been restored.

Martha House for prostitutes in Rome.[35] We organized a vast feeding program for the poor during the Roman famine of 1538 and 1539, when in the holy city the dying were lining the streets and starving children were wandering about. I did not lock the prostitutes into cloisters, as would have been the custom, but tried to educate them for an honorable life in the world and for marriage. I inspired the founding of a home for girls at risk and supported orphanages, a house for Jews and Moors[36] who wanted to become Catholic. It did not seem too "secular" to me to bring about reconciliation between Tivoli and Castel Madama,[37] to become

35 The Martha house was a refuge for women who had been forced into prostitution for economic reasons. It also housed victims of domestic violence. Women at the house were taught skills for securing alternative sources of employment, helping them prepare for marriage, or deciding whether or on what conditions to return to their husbands.

36 Both Jews and moors were considered minorities at the time, hence subject to derision and discrimination. It is significant that two of Ignatius's closest associates, Polanco and Laínez, were of Jewish descent, hence members of a minority group that was regarded by many office-holders in the church with contempt. When it came time for electing the third superior general, Polanco would have been the natural candidate to replace Laínez; however, heavy opposition from within and outside the order prevented the election of yet another Jesuit who was of Jewish descent, so that Borgia was elected.

37 At Paul III's request, Ignatius had gone in 1548 to the city of Tivoli to effect reconciliation between its residents and those of the neighboring Castel Madama. The fight was over toll

"socio-politically" active even in old age, just as I had done during the last visit in 1535 of my Basque homeland, where I stayed at the poorhouse of Azpeitia and ate with the poor what I had obtained through begging and where I drafted and put into practice for my native town a carefully planned ordinance on behalf of the poor. Yes, I also founded schools and made legal provisions for their foundation, thereby somewhat reluctantly adjusting the order's law of poverty. The result was that in some countries and at certain times the order became one of schools and schoolmasters, to which I in no way object, provided that thereby the overall character and mentality of the order is not distorted. Do not forget that in my time, these schools were run without charging tuition, hence had a socio-political aim, while your schools today are expensive for your students and they have to be, with which I concur. Much more could be said about all of that.

There is one thing I want to ask: Has the order largely forgotten this side of my life? If so, it may have been the result of historical necessity. As mentioned numerous times before, I do not expect that the history of the order be a mirror image of me. But does the order have to remain this way? Is it not possible that in the order's future something should spring to life that was important to me during my lifetime as I practiced

fees leveled by Tivoli and had resulted in fierce hostility and bloodshed. Ignatius's efforts settled the dispute.

discipleship of the poor and humble Jesus? Can the challenge of a new situation possibly lead to a dramatic change of the order's direction so it can remain faithful to its original intent? At your 32nd General Congregation of 1974 you have newly declared "the fight for faith and justice" as your task and you have admitted "with sorrow your failure in the service to the faith and to justice." You have understood engagement for justice in the world as an inherent and essential part of your mission, a part that is not simply a preferential addendum to your proclamation of the gospel. You have spoken of the "complete and entire liberation of the person that leads to participation in the life of God." I hope that you are serious about that. Of course, your historical and social context is completely different from the way mine was in the sixteenth century, where intentionally planned changes in society were not yet the duty and responsibility of a Christian's love of neighbor the way they are today. It seems to me, though, that if you were to take seriously the decisions of the 32nd General Congregation, your highest organ of authority, you would embark on a new future path of your singular and never-changing mission on which the one you call your father can accompany you in spirit, too.

What exactly such a struggle for more justice in the world will look like, I cannot foresee. By no means should you become everyday politicians, party officials, members of large socio-political organizations, and neither should you be mere theorists in the so-called Christian social sciences. Under no circumstances should you be seeking power in society or insist that by having more power one can serve one's neighbor better. That may be the underlying motto of actual politicians, who are justifying their profession and in part are speaking the truth, in part are lying. But it cannot be your motto, neither in secular society nor in the church, even if such power were to be within your reach.

If you practice the discipleship of the poor and humble Jesus, if you do not consider the newly arising and much greater marginalization that the future may impose on your life in society as a bitter force but can embrace it as Jesus' own lot, you may reach the place where your struggle for justice can truly happen. You really have no idea what type of marginalization it was within the ecclesiastical society, or should have been, when I and my first companions renounced the monastic garb and similar symbolic attestations of ecclesiastical status in society, even if up to now very little has come of it. Melchior Cano[38] has correctly said that

38 Melchior Cano (1525–1560) was born in Tarangon, Spain, and had joined the Dominicans at an early age at Salamanca. In 1546, Cano was appointed to the theological chair of that university. His reputation of great learning rests largely with a posthumous work, *De Locis theologicis* (1562), in which he seeks to free dogmatic theology of its vain subtleties of the schools and to bring it back to first

doing so meant a marginalization in ecclesiastical and sociological terms which should have been perceived as irreconcilable with the nature of an order that was ecclesiastically approved. It is similar to the way today's church feels toward priests who are working in the secular world. So, you can still do your advanced theology, develop cultural-political theories, engage in church politics, make your opinions heard in the mass media, and so on. All of this you may certainly do. But you should not gauge your life and the significance of the order on the successes in these areas.

If all you can do is acknowledge with sadness and resignation that this order did not regain the cultural, political, and ecclesiastical significance it had prior to its suppression in 1773, if this plain fact, which should not be covered up, fills you with sadness and secret resignation, then you have not understood in the least what you ought to be: people who by means of God are trying to forget themselves, those who are following the poor and humble Jesus, who are proclaiming his gospel, who are siding with the poor and marginalized in the struggle for gaining more justice for them. Are you no longer able to do that now and in the future? Does any of this depend on the power and glory that the Society of Jesus once had, or is such power in actuality a terrible danger since

principles. He does so by providing rules, methods, and a system of scientific treatment.

by it one loses God and seeks to pass over Jesus' own death? If apart from the mystery of God to whom alone you want to entrust yourselves unconditionally, there does not and should not exist anything else in the world and in history, inside and out, in heaven and on earth that one should aim for and love without reservations and unconditionally, is then not your own order that you love and its future among the things that should be calmly received when given to you and equally calmly released when taken away? Did I not say in my own time that in the event the order went under, all it would take me for recovering inner peace and closeness to God would be a maximum of ten minutes?

Looking to the future

In conclusion, I should like to say something about those who are not Jesuits. In the course of my life, I have had the dearest friends and companions within the order, but throughout life I also had many friends who were not Jesuits. There were the great and the small, the rich and the poor, the educated and the simple, along with good friends among those who were members of other orders, men and women. I never thought that everybody had to become a Jesuit. Certainly there were many for whom the experience of the exercises I gave resulted in a radical conversion and spiritual awakening; but they did not become Jesuits, even if the external circumstances would have allowed for it and could have been accomplished much easier than for someone like the viceroy Francis Borgia.[39] Of course, what I have said is a given, but it does not hurt to say it explicitly.

Any type of lifestyle and certainly the one that wishes to form a person from the very center within will invariably end up making the claim to universality, to general validity, so that one can easily detect in other Christian lifestyles the preliminary, the compromise, the falling short of radical principles in contrast to one's own. The result is that, at the most, one silently tolerates these as human shortcomings. Not seldom did you practice such an understandable and yet foolish overestimation of your own lifestyle in your history. Hence, the frequent criticism of Jesuits being prideful is well justified. However, when such an overestimation of one's own lifestyle, such a claim to universality, no longer holds true even in the eyes of the naïve due to concrete historical evidence to the contrary, the opposite danger springs up: One becomes uncertain about one's lifestyle, is no longer convinced that it is

39 Francis Borgia (1510–1572) was born near Valencia, Spain, and was made a member of the court of Charles V. In 1539, he was appointed by the emperor viceroy of Catalonia. When his wife died in 1546, he decided to join the Jesuits. After visiting with them at Rome, he returned to Spain in 1550 handing over his royal title and the entire estate to his son so that he could become a priest. He was ordained and joined the Jesuits the same year and in 1554 was appointed commissary general of the Jesuits in Spain.

unconditionally valid for oneself, even if it is not appropriate for all, and one begins looking for a "synthesis" of everything and all, thus producing nothing but a spineless mishmash that thinks itself progressive just because it has mixed together all that was of yesterday. However, those who have broken through to the infinite freedom of God do not need to appropriate everything there is and that could be in order to prevent internal insecurity. When one has modestly but firmly appropriated what is one's own, there is no worry about having to follow every new fad. One's future has to come from oneself.

I have strayed a little from the topic so as to exhort you Jesuits once more. What I wanted to say, though, is this: The world need not consist of people only that are Jesuits or of those who can be gauged by how similar they are to you or how dissimilar; and this is true even more so today. And yet: you basically have a mission to those who are not Jesuits and those not aspiring to be a smaller version of you. I used the word "basically" because one cannot calculate in advance the degree by which you will be able to reach them; it is a matter of hope, not calculation, and it occurs at the free discretion of the mysterious God of history. Basically then, you have a mission that can be of interest to anybody. In this regard I need to say something about all Christians and all people, even if what is of general importance will always appear only in a historical version, hence cannot apply to everyone. With this caveat, the things I tried to live by and say and the things I and my companions tried to teach people are still of overall significance.

Of course, one could say that I belong to those who stood at the threshold of the European "modern era" and, despite all the medieval customs I practiced and conveyed, that what was new and unique with me was typical for the modern era, an era that is now about to end, even if no one is quite sure what will come after that. One could say that my "spirituality" in its mystical individualism and its rational-psychological approach is typically modern, hence is coming to an end. One could say that nothing will change in this modern era with its individualistic subjectivity and rationality because it remains embedded in the incredible apparatus of the Roman church and is placed at the church's disposal, which is an even older apparatus, hence has even less of a chance at survival. But things are not that simple, at least not in the history of Christianity and the church, hence in matters of historical developments that occurred within the church's history and whose beginning did not simply imply a prognosis of death. But let us put the history of theology aside. All I am saying is this: In the church things do not quickly disintegrate just because they had their concrete origins in a certain era of the church's history.

My religious individualism that you call "modern" may once again be of great significance, and more so than ever, precisely because the people of "post-modernity" feel as if they are vanishing and going under in this organized mass culture. I am most certainly not opposed to your trying to discover the communal, the lived group experience, the base community and to find yourselves at home there in the religious and the interpersonal. But be cautious and sober. The individual will never find complete fulfillment in the group.

Solitude before God and being at home in his silent immediacy is indispensable to humans. If this became evident in the church at the start of the modern era, then this development belongs to the type of history that will not go under but will remain and will need to remain, also through you. Will there be people who will not pay any attention to the word "God," no matter what stage of life they are in? Will there be people who no longer ask about the inexplicable that lies beyond the infinite complexities? Will there be people who consistently and quite successfully prevent the ultimate mystery from drawing near them, even though it resides in them unnamed as the one and the all-encompassing, the primordial origin and the primordial goal, the one that allows us to lovingly say "You" when we have permitted ourselves to fall into its abyss and are thus being set free? What if one day something like that came to pass? I would not be shaken by it. It only would mean that human beings individually or as a whole had transmuted into clever animals and that the history of human freedom, responsibility, guilt, and forgiveness had come to an end; but since we Christians are anticipating an end already, it is only the type of end that would have changed. In spite of all that, people worthy to be called "human beings" would still be finding eternal life.

One can speak of God even in the future as long as one truly understands what is meant by this word. There will always be a mysticism and a mystagogy of the unspeakable closeness of this God, who has created the other at his initiative in order to give himself to the other in love as life eternal. It will always be possible to teach people to topple the finite images of idols that line their paths or to calmly walk past them, to consider nothing they encounter as absolute in regard to powers and principalities, ideologies, goals and futures of a distinct and certain kind, to remain "indifferent," to become "calm," and to experience in this seemingly empty freedom the true nature of God.

There will always be people who when gazing at Jesus the crucified and risen one dare to walk past all the idols of this world and become unconditionally open to the incomprehensibility of God as love and mercy. Their number in proportion to all of humanity is ultimately irrelevant, provided the church as the sacrament of the salvation of the entire world is present in it. There will always be people who gather in this faith in God and Jesus Christ in the church, thus forming, carrying, and enduring it, the church that is the historically tangible, institutional presence and which, to me, is given in the most concrete sense (and in the hardest and the most bitter, too) in the Roman Catholic Church.

As long as there are such people, I will always have

a mission to all people, even if this may sound haughty. For all I wanted to do was help people understand and comprehend what I have just now said. Ultimately, I did not want a unique program, nor a Christianity or spirituality of a special type, though I am aware, of course, that every human being can communicate that which is valid for all only in the way that is characteristic of him or her, hence never reaching everyone or even canceling oneself out when daring to proclaim the eternal God and his Christ. Thus, the question about the future influence of my life and my teachings is irrelevant. Silent vanishing could be the most admirable act because, regardless, God will always remain the ever greater one. May his name be blessed.

I have said many things. And yet I have forgotten much or left much unsaid that you or someone else had hoped to hear me address. And I will not even mention the other topics I could have addressed in the place of those that I did. Because the outcome would still be the same: the silence in which God's eternal praises are sung.

Index

About the Translator

Annemarie S. Kidder, Ph.D. is a German native speaker, professor at the Ecumenical Theo-logical Seminary, Detroit, and Presbyterian pastor. She is the author and editor of numerous books, among them a collection of Karl Rahner's sermons, prayers, and essays, titled *The Mystical Way in Everyday Life* (2010) and *Making Confession/Hearing Confession: A History of the Cure of Souls* (2010).